MW01045866

The Joys of ALS

Finding happiness in a dark place

Keith Slater

Questex

© Keith Slater 2015

ISBN 978-1512096248

Copying from this book in whole or in part (with the exception of brief extracts for the sole purpose of review) is forbidden by law, and all infringements will be prosecuted.

Library and Archives Canada Cataloguing in Publication

Slater, Keith, author
   The joys of ALS: finding happiness in a dark place / Keith Slater.

ISBN 978-1-5120-9624-8 (paperback)

   1. Slater, Keith. 2. Amyotrophic lateral sclerosis--Patients--Canada-- Biography. 3. Dramatists--Canada--Biography. 4. Married people--Canada--Biography. 5. Amyotrophic lateral sclerosis--Humour. I. Title.

RC406.A24S63 2015   362.1'968390092 C2015-903714-X

I dedicate this book to Rosalind, my dear wife.
She is my best friend and has loved me without once
faltering over the 58 years since I met her.
Her steadfast dedication now, literally, keeps me alive.

The front cover photograph shows me with most of my
family.

List of Contents

1   Introduction

"The *what?* The *joys* of ALS? *Joys!!* Are you serious? What are you, some kind of weirdo nut case who's been let out of the Funny Farm?"

Yes, I'm serious. And you heard right. You didn't misread the book title. I did indeed choose the word 'joys' and the choice was deliberate. And, to the best of my knowledge and belief, my mental state is firmly located well towards the saner end of the Genius / Lunatic spectrum.

From the book title, then, a few of my more intelligent readers may deduce, in a major feat of brilliant insght, that I am not giving them a dry, boring list of clinical symptoms of ALS or a detailed description of the degenerative changes that take place as the illness progresses. I am also, most emphatically, *not* writing a raging diatribe against God, life, unfairness or other such targets for fury. Nor is the book a pitiful, woe-is-me whine about all the hardship, mental and financial, inflicted on the suffering writer. All of these are well represented in the ALS literature and most of them, to my mind, are not very helpful.

What I intend to do instead is to present a light-hearted (well, within reason, given the subject!) personal account of the way in which one man (that's me, Keith) and his devoted wife (her name is Rosalind) faced squarely up to the challenges brought about in life by experiencing an illness regarded as horrendous by the vast majority of people. I plan to minimize the doom and gloom, concentrating instead on how to squeeze the maximum amount of fun and pleasure out of an unfortunate situation. There are times when this is difficult, or even virtually impossible, and I won't gloss over or ignore them, but I'll try to tell you how we've dealt with them. I realize that I may not survive long enough to complete the book, because the illness is so unpredictable, but I'm prepared to launch out on a risky venture of faith in an effort to do so. (If you're actually reading these words, though, you can be reasonably certain that I did!)

You'll notice that the only names I mention in the book are those of family members and a very few close friends who have supported us continually, essentially on a weekly basis, over the entire seven years since I was diagnosed. This omission of identification was a decision taken for two reasons. First, there have been so many people who have given us so much help and support in lesser but crucial ways that I couldn't name all of them individually. Nor would I want to leave anybody out, because I really value the tremendous contributions they have made to giving me a happier life. The second reason is more prosaic. Although the great majority of health care workers have been very good, there have been a few lemons and I've described some of the experiences I've suffered at their hands. I suspect that, if I identified them by name, one or two of them could try to sue me and I don't want to have to deal with that kind of problem, thank you!

A brief word about ALS might be worth mentioning at the outset. We know very little about it, but I've heard that it's supposedly contracted more readily by people who are extremely intelligent and have a physically active lifestyle. This is all very flattering, tending to imply that dim-minded slobs are compensated to some extent for the insults hurled at them from all sides by the rest of society. I'm also told that ALS is not a disease, since it's neither infectious nor contagious, but is thought to be triggered by some sort of trauma. All of these (with the possible exception of 'extremely intelligent' did I hear?) are very relevant in my own case, as you'll discover if you have enough patience to continue reading the book. It's apparently tricky to diagnose, because the symptoms can vary widely, possibly including many indicative of other illnesses. The effects range from loss of voluntary muscle function in different areas of the body, including limbs, fingers, tongue, neck and those used in controlling digestive, bladder or bowel function. It's progressive, irreversible and degenerative at a rate that varies widely (and apparently unpredictably) in each individual person. Mobility declines, at a rate determined by the way the illness progresses, with no currently known means of preventing it until the patient dies (an event which effectively resolves the situation!).

Thus, if you hope to find any useful help or guidance from this book, you must realize one crucially important fact: you need determination, strong will, a sense of humour and, most of all, a devoted, loving companion who is prepared to be a strong, determined advocate on your behalf to make sure that all your needs are met. If you find nothing else in the book, I trust that you will take away my foremost invariable rule.

I am *not* dying from ALS.

I am living *with* ALS.

2   Prelude to a diagnosis

Before embarking on the task of trying to explain how we manage to get our jollies in a situation that could be regarded by some people as grim, I believe I should provide you with brief details of our lives before ALS. This will explain to a good extent how we subsequently dealt with the situation we had to face.

Rosalind and I were both born in the Oldham area of Lancashire, a county in the North of England. Lancastrians are notorious for their black humour and native wit. From an early age, they learn that, if something unpleasant happens to you, your reply is to make a joke about it and get on with your life without letting the repercussions affect you. We were also brought up as Methodists, acquiring religious faith that stayed with us to sustain us throughout our lives.

After my doctorate in Textile Technology was finished at Leeds University, we emigrated to Canada, where I spent the rest of my career as a university professor. After retirement, I was granted Emeritus Professor status, providing me with a continuing position in the university. Part of my academic duties consisted of writing scientific books and articles, a task I enjoyed immensely. I have published twenty books of nonfiction, some 150 or so scientific journal articles, plus about the same number of papers presented at textile conferences in 45 or so different countries. In short, my career kept me rather busy.

Eventually, the repetitive occupation of churning out only nonfiction became a bit boring, so I decided to relieve the impending monotony by trying my hand at writing fiction. I produced over 120 short stories (ranging from excellent to quite good or OK, readers tell me) and a few novels (mediocre by modern standards in my opinion, though I believe they would have been regarded as reasonably good if I'd written them fifty years earlier).

Then, when I was about 40, Rosalind (who, unlike me, had been involved in amateur theatre before we married) persuaded me to read for a part in the next production at our local theatre. I got a small role (*"There are no small roles, only small actors"*) and I was instantly bitten by the acting bug. I became a regular cast member in at least one play a year and seemed to be very popular with audiences. Later, I tried my hand at directing and again was successful. In the 35 years we spent in theatre, I acted in about 80 shows and directed about 70. As we became more heavily involved, we both took on executive duties, including two spells each in the heavy task of filling the position of President. My next step was to combine my two favourite extramural activities of theatre and writing by turning out plays, with over 30 written at the moment.

As I skim through the paragraphs I've set down, I'm becoming uncomfortably aware that I seem to be in the middle of a bragging session. I assure you that this really isn't the purpose of my words. What I want to show you is that I fulfilled one of the factors leading to the tendency to suffer from ALS. It also gives an indication of why (as I'll describe later) the idea of having such a serious illness never crossed my mind.

The second relevant factor, the matter of physical activity, was also present. I'd been an enthusiastic sportsman throughout my life, taking part in games of cricket, football (soccer and rugby, that is), tennis (lawn and table), some of which I continued to play well into my sixties. Also, from my arrival in Canada, I'd been a member of the Cardiovascular Club, an exercise class devoted to maintaining a healthy heart in senior members of the university. We met every lunch time and, when the leader retired, I took his place for about 25 years.

Extensive travel, though I enjoyed it tremendously, also was tiring. In addition to wandering around the world to attend conferences, I spent time on sabbatical leave in a number of universities in Europe and was the academic director of two overseas semesters, in Paris and Guatemala, for my university. I shouldn't omit, too, the trips for pleasure. I organized half a dozen European holidays for friends, with up to about 30 people on each one, in countries where I spoke the language, as well as taking family holidays.

For the other suspected reason why ALS happens, trauma, you can take your pick of a couple of possibilities. I'd had the usual number of falls, bumps, etc., since childhood and on throughout my life, but I don't think these were severe enough to count for such a drastic effect. However, other events certainly were. In 2002, during a Caribbean holiday, I was cycling around the island and suddenly saw a drainage slot in front of me. Unable to stop in time, I gripped the handlebars tightly. I managed to avoid being thrown off, but agonising pain shot up both arms and I couldn't feed or dress myself for three days. Back in Canada, I found that the rotator cuffs in both shoulders were so badly damaged that no surgical repair was possible.

The second unpleasant traumatic episode took place in 2004. I was trundled off to hospital with some kind of urinary obstruction, which was quickly cured, though I didn't manage to escape before a urologist persuaded me to have a PSA test for prostate cancer. It was lucky that he grabbed me, because the test was positive, but he assured me that the cancer was completely contained, so surgery would be simple and rapid, with no problems.

He was wrong. First, he made a mistake and severed an artery. Rosalind had been told that she could come back to see me in the recovery room by one o'clock, but it was seven in the evening by the time I was conscious and five units of blood had been shoved into me to get me to that state. Two days later, I had three pulmonary embolisms, which didn't do much to improve my feelings of warmth towards the surgeon.

Well, having prepared you for the events that led to the diagnosis of ALS, I'll get on with my life story. For about two years, I experienced minor and, to my mind, unrelated symptoms. I was more tired than I had been, but I was getting older, having passed my biblically- allotted three score years and ten. That period happened to coincide with one of my spells as theatre president and I'd acted in three plays, as well as directing two more. In addition, I'd continued to lead the exercise class, organized one of my European walking holidays, and been forced to undergo radiation treatment because the prostate cancer had returned (doctors' assurances be hanged!). Hence, I thought, fatigue was not only reasonable, but virtually inevitable.

My voice, too, was less powerful than it had been, a change that I put down to age and too much projection at the theatre. My fine motor control of muscles was decreasing slightly as well. One of my theatrical roles was to play the part of an ugly sister in Cinderella. I had great difficulty in fastening up the tiny buttons on my clothes and needed a dresser for all my changes, not only the quick ones. The final straw of my otherwise brilliant portrayal came when I couldn't rip the sleeve out of Cinderella's dress, as required by the script. Rosalind, who was directing the show, thought I was clowning around and tore strips off me until I convicted her that my difficulty was genuine, whereupon she made changes to provide me with a better means of gripping the fabric. Again, we assumed that old age and overwork were the cause of the problem.

I'd also noticed that the flesh at the base of my right thumb had shrunk to the point where it had virtually gone and that I occasionally experienced slight trembling in the fingers of that hand. Once more, we laid the blame on the aging process and too much activity. It's hard to imagine, looking back, how I could have been such an innocent idiot, but the only excuse I can offer is that I was far too busy to worry about minor ailments of impending old age. I console myself now with the knowledge that it would have made no difference if I'd been aware of my condition because the illness is incurable and can't be prevented.

What eventually influenced me to make time to investigate was a TV show. We were watching a murder mystery and noticed that one of the characters, who had symptoms vaguely like mine, was suffering from ALS. We jokingly wondered why I hadn't been offered the role as I would have been much better for the part, then Rosalind told me that it might be a good idea to see a doctor, just to make sure that it wasn't something that I should be concerned about and I agreed to find an opportunity when I could fit it in. Our family doctor didn't appear too worried, but set up a few appointments with specialists for me. They could find nothing serious, confirming my impression that normal changes were the reason for my symptoms. I went to the last appointment, with a neurologist who was a casual friend from the local Rotary Club, expecting the same kind of response.

The date, forever etched in my mind afterwards, was June 10, 2008.

3   D-Day

"I'm so sorry, Keith, but I have bad news for you. You have ALS."

"Oh," was all I replied.

"I really am very sorry, but I have to advise you to get your affairs in order as soon as possible."

"Why? How much time have I got left?"

"Six months at the most."

"Oh. I see."

It had been a bit of a slapdash diagnosis, I remember thinking. He'd stuck a couple of electrodes into my thigh, one near either end, then applied a series of electrical pulses to one of them and measured the time it took for them to reach the other. He'd then disappeared into an inner sanctum for ten minutes to check the results against some standard tables, I assumed, before returning to deliver the completely unexpected bombshell. For all I knew, he could have been fortifying himself with a sip or two of adrenaline enhancement in case I turned nasty and decided to assault him.

Don't assault the messenger. The thought probably saved him. In truth, it made perfect sense to me. All the symptoms, fatigue, loss of voice and muscle control, etc., that I'd thought minor and unrelated, were part of the same illness and now easily accounted for.

(Some time later, when I was recounting the conversation to a close friend, I modified it by adding a few sentences of fictitious extra dialogue:

"I've got some good news for you, though."

11

"How on earth can you have any good news after a diagnosis like that?"

"Easy. You've got Alzheimer's. Go home and forget about it.")

The real conversation was very different. We spent a few minutes discussing the next steps and he eventually spoke a little hesitantly.

"You're taking the news very calmly, Keith."

"Didn't you just tell me there's no treatment to stop or slow down the deterioration?"

"Yes."

"Then I don't see much point in ranting, do you?"

I didn't tell him, but I already had quite a bit of acquaintance with the effects of ALS.

In the 1983-4 academic year, I was honoured with the award of a Visiting Fellowship at Gonville and Caius College in Cambridge University. As it happened, Stephen Hawking was a Fellow of the same College, so I came to know him quite well. He was not yet a familiar figure outside the Astronomy field, because his book *A Brief History of Time* was not then written, but he could still eat and speak, though with some difficulty, and was able to travel independently around Cambridge on his power chair. Rosalind also become friendly with Jane, his wife, at various College social events so we found out some of the difficulties they had to face as a result of the illness. In our wildest dreams, we never once remotely imagined that, thirty years later, we would have to face the same problems. One thing that impressed me enormously was the fact that all the people around him treated Stephen like any other human being, with no special arrangements to bring attention to his plight. The other fact I noticed was his wry humour, and the strong impression that these two memories left on me has greatly inspired me in my own situation.

With the appointment ended, I left the medical building and crossed the parking lot to my car. Before I reached it, I had made two resolutions. First, no doctor was going to tell me when I'd be dying. That was a matter for God and me to work out. My mother often said that *"God helps them that helps themselves"* and I fully intended to provide all the help I could in this very worthwhile endeavour. Secondly, if God happened to be on the same side as the neurologist, I didn't intend to waste what little time left to me by bemoaning my fate. Lancastrians don't follow the peculiarly North American habit of going through a mandatory grieving process and I certainly didn't want to start the standard sequence of denial, bargaining, etc. specified in Grief 101. I had an incurable degenerative sickness, so the best way of getting on with things was to proceed with my life and enjoy it to the best of my ability.

So much for the resolutions. My next task was to pass on the bad news to Rosalind.

She was, understandably, shattered. Like me, she'd been expecting a diagnosis of some trivial problem that could be ignored or cured by rest, simple treatment, etc. Her reaction was far more severe than mine and I was helpless in trying to console her. By chance, the phone rang and she picked it up without thinking. It was a Board member from the theatre and, as he launched into his request, he sensed the emotion in Rosalind's voice, stopped abruptly and asked what was wrong. When she blurted out the news, he stumbled over a few words of condolence and rang off without asking for the information he was seeking. Two hours later, his wife called back to tell us about a book she'd found on the Internet, written by a man who'd had the same diagnosis and was still alive twenty years later. The title of the book is *Eric is Winning,* by Eric Edney, and we ordered a copy immediately. It's an uplifting book, we found when it arrived, with many suggestions for treatments to help that didn't depend on the standard medical view of inevitable, rapid death and was our first hint that the situation might not be as hopeless as I'd been led to believe. I told Rosalind of my resolutions and she immediately agreed with my ideas. She promised that, if I would fight to stay with her for as long as I possibly could, she would devote her life to caring for me. As you will see if you read on, she has faithfully kept that promise without faltering, even for an instant, to this day. She has opened my eyes to a new view of what true love can mean; I owe my survival entirely to her single-minded dedication.

Two days later, after the neurologist phoned us to see him, we went for another appointment. He gave me a handbook about ALS, describing symptoms, progression, effects, etc., and informing me that people with the illness lasted for two to five years, maximum, but could die much more rapidly in severe types of the affliction (presumably including whatever type I had) from pneumonia or asphyxiation. I asked why Stephen Hawking was still alive and he told me there could be a mistaken diagnosis in such cases. Rosalind asked him if his own diagnosis could be mistaken and he assured her that he never had been wrong before. This, naturally, didn't do much in the way of providing her with ample comfort, so he tried to improve his image, telling us that he'd arranged for me to get a second opinion. He'd made an appointment for me with a famous specialist who was the head of an ALS clinic in Toronto. We thanked him but I pointed out that, since the date he'd booked was in January, it could become a bit redundant, since it was a month or so later than the time he'd established for my demise. He seemed somewhat flustered as he phoned the clinic to ask for an earlier appointment, with an attempt to explain why it was necessary.

We took pity on him and ended the meeting. In my usual tactful manner, I told him that I didn't think I would accept his diagnosis and intended to do my best to live life to the full, hopefully surviving long enough to read his obituary. He took my attempt at humour quite well, though he hasn't yet obliged me by dying.

There again, neither have I.

4   Early changes

Once we'd recovered from the fun and games of dealing with the unexpected diagnosis, it was time to look at the new plans we needed to make for the rest of our time together, taking into account its drastically reduced length. We'd been married for forty-nine years and were saddened by being cheated out of the chance to celebrate our Golden Wedding a year later, six months after my expiry date. We'd looked forward to it as it approached and had to adjust our thinking somewhat drastically.

My first plan was to continue the routine I'd been following for as long as I could. I used to walk over to the university each morning, spend a couple of hours in my office, where I was still writing academic papers, books and other stuff, then go to the gym to lead the exercise class. After that, I'd go home for lunch and spend the afternoon with Rosalind, either pottering round the house and garden or spending time away from home on a shopping or pleasure excursion. The evenings were often spent at the theatre, where one or both of us would usually be involved in a play or administrative duties. At the diagnosis time, Rosalind was acting in a play (an incredibly challenging task with such a load on her mind) which I, as well as being theatre president, was directing,. We decided to keep our news to ourselves until after the production ended and the last night party came to a rather subdued end when I made the announcement. For obvious reasons, there was no point in undertaking any long-term commitments, so I realized that I could never audition for a play from that time on. It was a bitter pill to swallow, but I consoled myself with the thought that at least I would never again have to suffer the disappointment of being rejected for a role! Despite the negative aspects of the illness, there were compensations if I looked for them; I learned a valuable lesson with that decision and I've found it very helpful ever since.

I continued to spend time at the university but, on the advice of our family doctor, began to use a walking stick when my balance became a bit less steady. The doctor also arranged for me to get a handicapped parking permit that I used, with some embarrassment at first, so I eventually began to drive to the university, saving about half an hour and some energy.

Then, in September, we had the first glimmer of hope that our situation might possibly not be quite as bad as we'd feared. The appointment with the ALS specialist took place and I didn't feel that half of the life remaining since my diagnosis had been used up. I walked into the clinic with a walking stick in case I needed it, though I didn't use it. The day was a long and arduous one. I registered, with a massive amount of information to be entered on a stack of forms, then waited for half an hour to be seen. The first session was with a young woman doing research on vocal changes. I spent an hour repeating consonants ten times each that resembled normal exercises used by actors to get the speech mechanisms working before going on stage. She made all kinds of complicated measurements on apparatus in or around my mouth to find what pressures and movements accompanied my great oratorical feat. I hope her research has yielded useful results, but I must regretfully admit to some slight doubts about the effectiveness of measurements that are subject to so many variables.

After another series of lengthy waits, I saw several junior staff members in turn. They each carried out tests of neural transmission rates in various parts of my body and focused on symptoms I experienced. More people conducted extensive blood tests, MRI scans and checks of my balance, etc. At last came the interview with the head of the unit. He told me that the initial diagnosis was correct, so I asked him if this meant that the prognosis was also correct. He said the test results seemed to indicate that I should have the normal two-to-five years of survival time from diagnosis and that he didn't need to see me for six months. Then he mentioned an experimental drug, Rilutek, which could prolong life for a few months in ALS patients. We discussed side effects, the main one of concern being potential liver damage that had to be checked by monthly blood tests. I felt that I didn't want to be involved in the trial and he entirely agreed with my decision, so I went to book my next appointment at the office before leaving. When that was done, the office manager, who appeared to be treated with awe by everybody from the head of the clinic down to the deputy assistant cleaning lady, began to prepare my Rilutek schedule. When I told her that I wouldn't be taking it, she bristled with indignation and informed me that all their patients took it. I stuck to my guns and was treated to a tirade of reasons why I was wrong and how all the patients swore by it. She became more and more angry as I countered all her list of reasons for taking the drug with reasons why I shouldn't. I didn't see why a glorified secretary should question the decision made by a patient and agreed by a doctor, so we left the clinic with furious vibes following us. I rather enjoyed those few minutes!

We returned home in a much more optimistic state of mind. It had been a long day, eight hours from leaving home to returning, but a worthwhile one. We could cautiously begin to plan for a slightly longer life expectancy, but we decided not to aim too high for fear of disappointment. After all, everything depended on who was right, the neurologist or (as we fervently hoped!) the specialist. In particular, we both agreed that it would be pointless to make any plans for our Golden Wedding until we were in a position of greater chance of success.

So I continued my daily routine until winter, with its severe cold, snow and icy roads, made conditions unpleasant, or even dangerous, for too much walking in my unsteady state. I exchanged my stick for a pair of Nordic walking poles, given to me by the group I led in Austria on one of the walking tours, which made me look far more athletic than I felt. At that time also, I wrapped up the incomplete projects I had at the university and started doing my academic work at home on most mornings, just driving to the exercise class. My friends there would open the side entrance to the building (contrary to security regulations) to shorten the walk from the parking lot and cut out the climb up a flight of fifteen concrete steps. The gym staff found me a vaulting horse base of the right height for me to have an occasional rest, though I continued to lead the exercises and take part in virtually all of them.

Spring also brought the second visit to the ALS clinic, with the same battery of tests. I felt that, with one notable exception, people there were significantly more friendly than on my first visit. The junior support staff in particular seemed to go out of their way to bestow broad, but surreptitious, grins on me and I wondered briefly, in passing, if I'd acquired some kind of notoriety by defying the office manager's determination to have me destroy my liver with Rilutek. She was the notable exception, addressing me with a carefully-controlled iciness, but making no reference to the topic of our disagreement. I gathered from various casual conversations that the great majority of patients had obeyed orders, so perhaps my fame had been achieved by my heroic stand against a tyrant. At any rate, the results of the tests were quite encouraging, because they showed very little deterioration and we realized that our dream of Golden Wedding celebrations might be possible after all.

So we hesitated for a few days and then determined to take the plunge. There would be two parties, we decided, one on the actual date of our anniversary in our home town of Oldham, England, for family and old friends and one after our return to Canada for those we had made since our emigration. Once the decision was taken, we set about the task of booking venues, inviting guests and organizing travel arrangements. Our wish was going to be granted, we thought, and dismissed all doubts from our minds!

5   Golden Wedding

The celebrations began with a minor setback. Our late evening flight from Toronto to Manchester was unable to take off because of technical problems. Luckily, we'd planned to spend a few days in England for a holiday before the party, so we had time to spare. The airline put us into the airport hotel and told us to check on the revised take-off time at eight o'clock the next morning.

The news was not encouraging. Another plane was needed and its arrival time wasn't yet known. On the previous night, fortunately, I'd contacted the hotel we'd booked, advising them of our situation. They'd agreed to keep our room available and left keys, with directions for reaching them in a hidden cupboard in case we arrived in the night. Thus, the continuing announcements of delays didn't worry us unduly, though we were thankful when we finally took off in the early evening.

After an uneventful flight, we landed in Manchester at an unearthly early hour of the morning and faced the next challenge. We headed to the car rental car office to claim our vehicle, but I was a bit perturbed to find out that I had to drive down six floors on a spiral ramp with a very small radius. I have to admit that, before we were halfway down, the combination of jet fatigue, weak arms and vertigo did make me wonder if we'd made a serious mistake. However, Rosalind doesn't drive cars with manual transmission, especially on the left side of the road, so I didn't really have much choice.

22

Once I was on normal roads, though, all driving problems vanished and never reappeared throughout the entire trip. We arrived at our hotel in Buxton, followed the instructions waiting as promised and collapsed into bed for four hours until breakfast time and woke up, rested and refreshed, for a hearty meal that brought us back to life.

Buxton is a medium-sized spa town at the eastern end of the Derbyshire Peak District and the ideal choice for a couple of days to recover from the flight. I'd never been to the place before, although I'd hiked in the Peaks dozens of times, but Rosalind knew it reasonably well because her father's family was from Derbyshire. I complimented her for suggesting the town and we spent two happy days wandering casually around the parks and stately houses, shops, etc.

Then it was time to set off for our trip round the area. We'd planned to stay for two nights at each of three villages, in different parts of the county, to minimize driving time to places of interest each day, but that went by the board very quickly. On the way to the first one, we saw a sign showing a side road to Tideswell, the village where Rosalind's family had lived and decided on a quick detour to see it. When we got there, we found that it was the week of the annual fair known as well-dressing. At the local inn, the 'Horse and Jockey', we asked the landlord if he had a room available and, when he told us he'd just had a cancellation that had left one free, we immediately decided to take it and make Tideswell our centre for the first two days. Next morning, on an excursion round the local sights, we were surprised to find that, in the years since our last time there, all the roads had shrunk so much that we could reach any of the spots we'd planned to see in well under an hour, so it made no sense to shift lodgings. A check with the landlord that the room was ours for the week if we wanted it was all we needed to change our plans from a three-centre holiday to a fixed-base one.

The stay was wonderful. When he saw me struggling with my walking poles, the landlord provided us with access from outside through a private door that allowed us to avoid a steep, narrow staircase that would have been a major challenge for a mountain goat. The food was plain but superb, inexpensive and plentiful. During the week, we met a number of people who had been friends with members of Rosalind's family and she spent many happy hours chatting with them and sharing memories. We went to the Methodist chapel on the Sunday to bring back glimpses of our young lives and saw even more of the Peak District than we'd hoped. Special thrills were trips to a few stately homes (for Rosalind) and the Blue John mine (for me). It has been a source of semi-precious stones for centuries and was a tremendous challenge for me. It was a very long and arduous journey of over a kilometre to travel around the steep, uneven floor of the cave with my walking poles and I had a real sense of achievement after completing it.

All too soon, it was time to get to the next part of our holiday. I added to the hotel bill a tip that I thought reasonably good, but must have been regarded as generous because the landlord asked if I was sure I wanted to make it that much and all the staff turned out to wave goodbye. Then, on July 2, off we set on the journey to Oldham and our longed-for party.

We decided to avoid the busy main roads, filled with heavy traffic, in favour of small local ones that wended their way through the countryside. We were in no hurry and meandered past the streams, rivers, reservoirs and small lakes of northern Derbyshire, with happy memories filling our minds, before stopping for a picnic lunch. Continuing northwards, we eventually arrived in the Yorkshire moors above Saddleworth, another haunt of younger days and familiar to viewers of various British TV shows. At the far end, we descended into the village of Delph, on the same outskirts of Oldham, and arrived at our destination, a charming hotel with a lovely view over the moors.

The next morning, we drove round a few other villages to bring more memories flooding back, returning to the hotel in time for a tasty lunch. In the afternoon, we'd arranged to be around to meet a photographer from the local newspaper, because they were running the story of our return home to celebrate our Golden Wedding. He skilfully managed to pose us so that my disabled state didn't show and sent some excellent copies of his shots. Afterwards, we entertained my cousin and his wife to afternoon tea, as she was unable to be with us at the party next day. The tea was far too huge for us to eat but, fortunately, our youngest daughter, Keirsten, and her husband, Stephen, with their offspring (too old to be called children!) arrived from Cardiff, where they had lived for over twenty years. All three grandchildren have great appetites and the food disappeared in no time. Keirsten and family were staying overnight because of the distance from Cardiff, so we had an evening of dinner and chatting.

Next day, the actual anniversary date of July 4, our guests arrived well in advance of the time arranged for lunch to start. They included, apart from Keirsten's family and Rosalind's sister Doreen, aunts, cousins and old friends, some of whom we hadn't seen since our actual wedding. Animated conversations went on ceaselessly before, during and after lunch as the food and wine brought out so many happy memories. There were over forty of us in the room, but it seemed as if we had more than double that number. Nobody wanted to leave, though many of them were well over eighty. At around four o'clock, the hotel manager gently reminded me that they had a wedding reception to handle at six and needed time to prepare for it. We all took the news in our stride and merely moved into a different room generously provided for us. At five o'clock, Keirsten reluctantly told us that they had leave to make the six-hour journey back to Cardiff and arrive home at a reasonable time. Gradually, other people began to drift away, but it was seven by the time we said goodbye to our last guests and were able to depart, glowing with pleasure, on the next phase of our adventures.

On our wedding day, we'd set off after the reception on a road trip to Cornwall for a couple of weeks and we planned now to repeat that journey. We knew we couldn't exactly follow the original route, because some of the small towns where we'd stayed were now much bigger and crammed with snarled traffic. On the first night, a couple of hours after leaving the reception hotel, we pulled into a motel at a rest area of the motorway for a tormented night. The room was stifling hot from faulty air and windows that were sealed shut, so we had no sleep. Next morning, when the receptionist asked the usual routine question, he heard about the problem and immediately offered to refund our accommodation charge. We gathered that it wasn't his first complaint and accepted his offer.

We resumed our journey, staying in two of the same towns of our honeymoon trip before reaching St. Ives, our destination fifty years earlier. We drove down into the crowded town along twisted, narrow streets and managed to get to the harbour, where we found a parking spot. We saw at once that it would be impossible to stay there. What had been a charming little village with an artists' colony when we were last there had become a tourist resort crammed with sightseeing crowded streets. They left no room for walking safely, let alone driving, with cobbled roadways that I found almost impossible to negotiate, with the combination of endless traffic and the difficulty of using my walking poles. We spent a pleasant day there, then drove along to next village, Carbis Bay, to stay for a few nights.

Then we wended our way back on the return leg of the trip, spending four days in Babbacombe, a resort that had been regarded as a very salubrious place in our youth but now appeared to have become a rather shabby and faded hideaway for old people. Even in my disabled state, I felt more alive and healthy than most of the people shuffling around the town. Our most enjoyable day was spent with a childhood friend and her husband, who had been at our wedding but couldn't get to Oldham for the 50th anniversary party because of distance. When we continued our homeward drive, we passed a sign indicating the road to Cheddar, famous as the origin of the well-known cheese, but regretfully felt that we didn't have time to stop there. A couple of days later, we reached the Deanwater Hotel, the same one where we'd stayed on our wedding night, and wallowed in memories in a lovely room and over a great dinner.

Back in Canada, we finalized the arrangements for our second party. We'd already booked the venue, a building set in the Arboretum at the university, with catering included, together with a Big Band specialising in music from the 1950's. All that remained was to do a final check on numbers and menu items with the university's catering staff, informing them that about 120 to 130 guests would be attending. We were so delighted, and honoured, when Roy, my roommate at university and best man at our wedding, came over from England to join the celebration. He stayed at our home for a few days before and after the party and we enjoyed many laughs as we reminisced.

The event was even more memorable and happy than we'd hoped. We allowed half an hour for chatting, followed by the buffet meal, an excellent one with a menu we'd chosen with the catering manager. Entertainment in the form of stories about our life then began. I'd asked ten of our closest friends to speak, but told them they had to focus on good times from the past and not dwell on any aspects of gloomy prognostications. The result was hilarious. Roy, as the person who'd known us longest, started by harking back to funny stories from university days and the wedding itself. He was followed by people from the theatre, the church, my exercise class and friends amongst the neighbours or with other connections to us, including my favourite student of all time. They did a splendid job, after which I gave a speech that earned me many compliments. (I thought it would be my last one, but I had another in me, as you'll find out if you struggle through the rest of this book). After hobbling across the room on my poles, I had to support myself by leaning against the platform used by the band, but I felt that the pose gave me a rather cavalier air.

Then the music started. I'd argued against booking a band, on the principle that it would make me miserable to see everybody dancing when we couldn't join in what had been one of our favourite activities. Rosalind, however, insisted and we added the cost of renting a temporary dance floor to the bill. I can't tell you how right she was and how much I'd been mistaken. Despite the need to stagger round the room on my poles, I managed to dance not only with her but also with each of our three daughters and our two oldest granddaughters. The technique I used was to leave my poles at a convenient chair, have the dance, then steer my partner back to the chair to retrieve them. With reluctance, I spared our youngest granddaughter the ordeal because I had to lean on my partners to some extent and I didn't think it was fair to expect a seven-year-old girl to risk the chance of collapsing under somebody of about four times her weight.

So the occasion was over and we'd pulled off a double celebration of the Golden Wedding we'd never expected to see. We learned a valuable lesson at the same time; never accept the pronouncements of medical 'experts' at face value. We've questioned every single one of them since then!

6   Holidays

The outstanding success of the trip to England for our Golden Wedding spurred us to consider more travel plans. The main question was whether we could afford it after the expense we'd already met for the two celebrations. We'd always been frugal travellers, though. In the first walking holiday I'd organized, for 30 friends from church, university and theatre, I'd kept the cost of a two-week holiday in the Rhein Valley down to $1600 per person from door to door, including return air fare, accommodation with breakfast and dinner, plus all ground transportation. So we decided to scrape together enough to travel as much as we possibly could while we had the chance, knowing that the day would soon come when we'd be unable to get away from home together ever again.

Before Keirsten and her family had gone back to Wales after the second party, then, we asked them if they could tolerate a visit from us in autumn. They were enthusiastic about the idea and we arranged to go to Cardiff so we could all have a week together during the midterm break. The Rhein Valley was an obvious destination and we had a great time taking daily trips by boat or train along the river from Rüdesheim, where we had riverside rooms with a lovely view over the passing vessels.

The week provided plenty of both pleasure and challenge. Our excursions took us to the quaint old villages on the banks of the river and inland, but the trips to vineyards and castles were the highlights of the holiday. We had a wine tasting at Shloss

Johannisberg, famous for the quality of its products and bought a bottle or two to take back to Wales. On one memorable day, we visited a castle built on the steep side of the slopes of the Rhein that involved climbing several very long flights of steps and, though it was a slow process with heavy dependence on my walking poles, I finally conquered the climb and the safe descent back to the boat dock for the return voyage, exhausted but with a feeling of triumph.

Each evening was filled with walks around the town to find restaurants, a different one every time, where we could enjoy a leisurely dinner before going back to the hotel for a leisurely chat to make plans for the next day. Although I was able to negotiate the steep streets of the town, it was obvious that I was slowing down the rest of the family and, when we returned to Cardiff, Stephen found a shop where he was able to rent a wheelchair for the rest of our time in Wales. I used it as a walker by pushing it along from behind until I was tired, then hopping in to be trundled about by somebody else. We took it with us to Weston-super-Mare for a week to get out of the way while the family got back into routine after the midterm break. It's a flat seafront resort and we made the most of it to have a wonderfully relaxing rest and recover from the German trip. We had absolutely no problems in travelling, because the trains and stations in Britain are fully accessible for wheelchairs. There was a station on a local branch line, five minutes' walk from Keirsten's house, from where it was possible to reach anywhere in Britain.

When the time came to return to Canada, we all made a spur-of-the-minute decision that we would try to go back to Wales for Christmas if we could find enough money to meet the cost. It was an ideal year to go, because Diane and Hilary would be away from Canada on holiday, so we'd have been spending the holiday alone. As added incentive, we knew that we'd have a wonderful time. Keirsten has always been a great enthusiast about celebrations and Christmas at her house was invariably full of excitement about the carolling, gift wrapping or opening games and, above all, the food.

Needless to say, we scraped together enough to make the journey. This time, Diane and Robert had lent us a wheelchair from their business to take with us. For the flight, the best way to take off from Toronto and land in Cardiff was to fly by KLM with a six-hour stopover in Amsterdam, where it was very useful. As expected, the holiday was wonderful. Keirsten excelled even her own high standards of enjoyment and all the family, plus numerous friends, were hauled willy-nilly into the celebrations. We took a few excursions, either by car to local places of interest or by ourselves on trains up into the Welsh valleys. We also spent a few days in Bath, the well-known spa town with its Roman antiquities and magnificent buildings. From there, we took the train to Cheddar, bypassed regretfully on our Golden Wedding excursion, to visit the famous cave. I was still able to walk a little by pushing the wheelchair and we managed to get round the cave. It had been used for centuries to store Cheddar cheese for ripening and we bought a whole one, at a very reasonable price, to take back for Keirsten. The most impressive part of the day was seeing Cheddar Man, a ten-thousand-year old skeleton shown by DNA analysis to be a direct ancestor of a present-day resident of the village.

Eventually, the time came for us to return to Canada, but an unfortunate mishap brought about a sad end to the holiday. When we checked in at Cardiff airport, the first leg of our journey, the short flight to Amsterdam, had been cancelled. After some initial confusion, the staff decided to send us by taxi to Heathrow and put us on an Air Canada flight to Toronto, all paid for by KLM. That was fine by us, especially when we found out that we'd been given first class seats, but our pleasure was shattered by the first sharp reminder of what ALS could eventually inflict on me. As our taxi stopped, I jumped out without noticing that a film of black ice had spread over the entire area. I fell forward and, because the ALS had paralyzed my arms, was unable to save myself, so smashed my face into the ground. The paramedic who arrived wanted to send me to hospital, but I refused; I'd no intention of risking the loss of our luxury seats! So I spent the day in pain behind a bandaged face, in the lounge at the airport then lying in a pod on the flight, unable to share Rosalind's enjoyment of the delectable food served. At the hospital where I went when we got back to Canada, I found that two small bones of my face were broken, but the surgeon recommended leaving them as long as I had no permanent pain, so I took his advice and have had no cause to regret the decision yet.

We must have been bitten by the travel bug quite badly, because we were off again in the spring for a trip that contained both curse and blessing features. We heard of an all-inclusive holiday opportunity in Cuba, our favourite Caribbean destination, at a resort that featured handicapped access facilities, with a very reasonable price for a ten-day stay. It was excellent, with good accommodation and food, but two events took place to cause concern for us.

The first was unavoidable. Twice a week, there was a mass effort to reduce the mosquito population by fogging the whole resort with a blanket spraying of insecticide without any warning. We fled to our room as soon as we realized what was happening and stuffed the gaps under our door and round windows with towels, but it was impossible to prevent some of the toxic fumes from getting into my lungs.

Then I had an accident that I should have avoided. As I pushed the wheelchair along a path, I failed to notice a small rock and tripped over it. This time I didn't injure my face, because I hung on to handles, but I cut my knee and had to go to the first aid office to have the wound bandaged. Before I realized it, the nurse had poured mercurochrome, a toxic antibiotic banned in North America because it caused mercury poisoning, on the wound. Now, one of the factors identified by Eric Edney in his book *Eric is Winning* as causing or exacerbating ALS is the ingestion of toxins, especially heavy metals, of which he particularly emphasizes mercury. I don't entirely agree with all his ideas, but I have no argument with this one. I had followed his recommendation to have all thirteen of the amalgam fillings in my teeth removed without the use of anaesthetics and here I was, loading my body up with one of the worst toxins I could have chosen. I desperately needed some help and, as I was to discover, the Cuban holiday was going to provide a kind of blessing that would bring it in some small measure. Though we didn't know it at the time, it was to be our final holiday.

7 Progression

When we arrived home from Cuba, I was at a fairly low ebb, unusually so for me. I was worried about the amount of toxins I may have absorbed, especially after having gone to the trouble (not to mention pain and cost) of having what seemed like half of the tooth mass inside my head hauled out. We realized that we ought to do something, but weren't sure what. Then we had the idea of seeing a naturopathic doctor for advice. She ran tests that confirmed the presence of high mercury levels in my body and told me that she didn't have the necessary means of removing the toxic metal. She referred me to a doctor in another town who practised both traditional and naturopathic medicine. He was very busy and couldn't give me an appointment until August.

In the meantime we had to take stock of the situation. I was still writing and leading the exercise class, but I worked at home and wasn't doing many of the exercises, sitting instead on my perch for virtually the entire class. I'd given up driving a year previously because I felt that I didn't have enough strength or control in my arm muscles to handle the steering in an emergency, so Rosalind had been driving me to and from the side door of the gym since the onset of the wintry weather and continued to do so even after the warm days arrived. We still had plenty of fun in the class. I'd introduced a special set of games for a change in routine, working on the principle that I decided the winning team before the game started and it then continued, with the rules being 'adjusted' by me, until the correct result was achieved. This brought great hilarity, particularly when my bending of the rules was a little too blatant, that cheered me up considerably and made the effort of getting to the class well worthwhile.

We managed to get to various other places, such as church, theatre performances, the market or nearby towns, without too much stress for Rosalind, a true hero, to handle. Thus, life continued, not quite normally but at least tolerably. My muscles were getting noticeably less reliable, though I was still talking, moving with the aid of support, and having quite an enjoyable life, considering the state I was in.

The time came to see the doctor about the mercury and his first step was to measure the actual level of contamination. It was a surprise to discover, from his test results, that I had a much more alarming problem, the presence of excessive amounts of lead in my body. On the linear scale he was using, the maximum safe level is 2 and any higher reading is dangerous. A reading of 20 is regarded as a potentially fatal dose. My level was slightly over 70 and his tests indicated that it had been at that value for many years. The doctor had never seen, or even heard of, anybody still being alive in such a state. He also found that I had comparable levels of cadmium and mercury, with lower, but still very dangerous, amounts of several other toxic heavy metals in my system. I have no inkling of where they came from, or how I had managed to survive for all that time with these things clanking around inside me, but I obviously had to do something about the situation. He set up a course of chelation treatments to remove the contamination and I embarked on them immediately. I was hoping that removal of the poisons would allow my body to recover some of its lost functioning, but the hope was in vain. The course of treatments took almost a year and reduced all the heavy metal readings to zero, but the symptoms characteristic of ALS remained unaffected and I continued to deteriorate.

I lost more and more mobility. Everywhere I went needed a walker that had to be packed in the car and hauled out (by Rosalind yet again, of course!) before I could be helped to leave the car. For shorter journeys, Diane and Robert found a power chair from their mobility store and I was able to zip around to church, shops and, on occasion, my university office or exercise class, which would take place outdoors in good weather so I could continue to lead it. Other inconvenient symptoms included some problems with breathing and swallowing. These, naturally, caused my eating ability to decline to the point at which I had to be careful about what, and how fast, I could eat. As I have always been very fond of my food, you will appreciate that this restriction didn't greatly please me!

Then came the first in a series of incidents that would bring a drastic change in my life. We were in a church service and I suddenly had an attack of intense breathlessness. I had to get outside into the fresh air and we left hurriedly. After a few minutes, I was fully recovered, but Rosalind decided that I wasn't riding home by myself. As usual, I'd gone to church on my power chair and she'd driven because I moved too quickly for her to keep up with me on foot, so she asked a friend to drive our car to our house and walked beside me while I travelled at a very staid pace.

We thought no more about it and continued to function in our usual way for a couple of months, until a second incidence, much more severe, happened. By chance, we were right outside the doctor's office and I was in an ambulance within a very short time, with an oxygen mask slapped over my face, leaving my chair to be picked up later. At the hospital, they shoved a suction tube down my throat and had the problem solved in no time, but kept me there overnight to make sure that I was fine. I was and went home next morning.

The third episode occurred the next week, at home in the late evening and was even more severe. So off I went in the ambulance again, oxygen pouring into my lungs, without being completely aware of what was happening. My most vivid memory is of a doctor bellowing in our faces.

"Are you DNR?"

I didn't reply, he turned his attention to Rosalind.

"Is he DNR?"

Neither of us had any clue about what he meant.

"I don't know," she said. "But he can't breathe!"

"I can see that, but is he DNR? He needs to decide right now! Or you do if he can't tell me."

Rosalind was almost in tears at the barrage of   shouting.

"What do you mean?"

"DNR. Do not resuscitate." He was almost screaming the words in her face by this time.

"No, of course he isn't! Get him breathing!"

I was rushed away, leaving Rosalind to pick up the shreds of clothing they'd hacked off me. Somebody shoved a suction tube down my throat and I was breathing normally within minutes.

The staff wanted to admit me to do some more intensive work on the problem. We realized that my situation was a serious one and readily agreed, so I was given a bed in ICU (we'd learned the jargon by this time, but its name had been changed from Intensive Care Unit to something else I can't remember, so I was wrong again!) with an emergency call button near my hand and Rosalind went home with worries about how long we still had together.

Next morning, she was back and, unfortunately, was confronted by Dr. Obnoxious again. She was ready for him this time.

"He'll have to have a tracheotomy. If you want to talk it over with him, I'll come back for your decision in ten minutes."

"We won't have made one by then," she told him calmly. "We need to discuss it with Keith's respirologist and we'll make an informed decision after that."

He was staggered. I suspect that nobody had ever stood up to his bullying manner before and he was at a loss for words. He didn't know it at the time, but he (and one or two other people) would be crossing swords again with Rosalind several times in the future. None of them would ever manage to beat her.

8   Crossing the Rubicon

The Rubicon was a river marking the northern boundary of the Roman Empire two millennia ago. When Hannibal, a general who had vowed to destroy Rome, reached its banks, he had a crucial decision to make. He could either withdraw and avoid a fight, or cross the boundary and begin a war that would lead to a great victory or to his defeat and death. The main consideration was that, if he crossed the Rubicon, there was no possibility of turning back.

I felt in much the same position after we'd discussed my situation with my respirologist. It was clear that the relatively carefree days were over and that we'd have to work a bit harder to get our laughs from that point on. I didn't know all that a tracheotomy entailed and found out that I would also need to have a gastric feeding arrangement (known as a G-tube) inserted to prevent the act of swallowing food from choking me. In addition, I needed ventilation equipment to push air into my lungs and allow the waste gases to be exhaled from them.

A couple of days later, after discussion with my respirologist, I took the plunge and told the obnoxious doctor that I would be having a tracheotomy. He booked a surgeon for the next day, presumably in case I decided to try swimming back across the Rubicon. The first operation had to be the insertion of the G-tube, to eliminate any risk of choking if I tried to swallow any food after the tracheostomy was in my throat (the surgical operation is a ***tracheotomy*** and the breathing tube inserted is a ***tracheostomy***, with an abbreviation 'trach', pronounced 'trake', normally being used). Since the G-tube procedure was going to be carried out in my room, using only a local anaesthetic, Rosalind decided to stay there to watch. The senior nurse told her that the surgeon wouldn't allow any observers, but she politely asked him for permission and overcame all his objections with logical answers until he recognised defeat and stuck her out of the way in a corner of the room. She watched, fascinated, as the camera I'd had to gulp down displayed the process taking place inside my body and regaled me with a detailed description several times subsequently.

All went well and a few days later, when observation showed that the G-tube was functioning properly, the second operation could be carried out. This one had to be done in an operating theatre under full anaesthetic, so she realized that it would not be reasonable to expect to be allowed to observe and didn't bother to ask. Again, there were no complications and I was trundled back to my room in ICU (or whatever the correct initials are!) to recuperate. And that's when the problems really began.

I was to spend the next eight weeks in that room and they were the worst time of my life. Not for want of care, I must emphasize. The nurses couldn't have done more for me. They met my every need, despite being overworked, and helped me to be comfortable and content as far as they possibly could, going well beyond the call of duty. The more senior medical and administrative staff were the people Rosalind had to fight. I was given an IV tube to get nutrients into my body and prevent dehydration, but I then swelled up like a balloon, especially in soft tissue areas (and I leave to your imagination the location of the immense imitation football that I developed), so I needed a diuretic to resolve the problem. As the liquid input was not reduced, my swelling didn't go down (with many ribald comments!) until, after two weeks, we pointed out that I was now feeding through the G-tube and could perhaps do without the IV tube and diuretic. They agreed and I gradually subsided, though I was still forced to keep a catheter installed.

We also got rid of another problem, the habit of overdosing me with drugs. I had to take a sleeping pill each night 'because all our patients have them' and a dose of something to calm me when I was 'under too much stress' until we objected to spending my entire time in a semi-conscious stupor. Rosalind finally ordered the nurses to ignore instructions from the doctor and only give me medication when I asked for it. The doctor was (understandably, he felt) quite put out and protested strongly, but Rosalind dealt with him calmly and refused to give in. He also had the habit of taking her outside my room to discuss my condition or treatment, until she pointed out that, despite being unable to speak or move, I was still in possession of all my mental faculties and more able to understand what he said better than she could. Eventually, he respected her and began to defer to her when she expressed her views and almost always accepted any decision she took from that time until my discharge, which amused me greatly.

44

In one area, we failed miserably. I'd always been very much active throughout my life and I asked to have exercises once I was down to a reasonable size. I got virtually nothing from the physiotherapist. He took one look at me, glanced briefly at my file and immediately classified me as beyond hope of any improvement in physical state. When we insisted, he grudgingly appeared twice a week, with no appointment or warning, to transfer me to a chair or change the settings on my hospital bed so I could sit up. He would return three hours later to get me back into my prone position in bed and was always too busy to spend time on range of motion exercises with me. As I saw him wandering aimlessly round the hall outside my room, coffee cup in hand, for much of every day, I doubted this, but my nurses often spared a little time to help me exercise. The obvious conclusion was that he regarded me as a waste of time, so was not interested in giving me any help.

After two weeks there, I began to ask how long my total hospital stay would last. The answers were very vague and it was gradually becoming obvious that the staff didn't intend to release me except to a long-term care facility. When we realized this, Rosalind immediately told the administrative staff that she would be taking me home and caring for me herself. They raised every conceivable objection, the most valid one (since they weren't allowed to say she was too old to cope with the task, though they clearly thought it) being that she would 'burn out' under the stress. She said bluntly that she was a Lancastrian and the term wasn't in her vocabulary. Then they changed tack, telling her that she couldn't take me home, because she didn't have the necessary training, to which she countered with the request that they should stop wasting time in argument and start teaching her.

They did and she was a superb pupil, so much so that the nurses training her were amazed at her speedy rate of progress. Nevertheless, obstacles continued to appear. A planning committee was set up, supposedly to establish the date for my discharge and the steps needed to get there. We soon realized that it was a smokescreen concealing their determination to prevent Rosalind from taking me home. It consisted of the doctor, a couple of nurses and the administrative heads of the relevant departments. Their aim, in general, was to keep me there, while Rosalind's was to establish a firm date for discharge.

She faced up to them in a determined fashion. They didn't stand a chance! My hospital records were presented for discussion. I'd refused to take my medication. On the contrary, she said. I'd taken any necessary drugs, but insisted on lower dosages because the amounts I'd been given initially left me half-conscious for up to 36 hours. I'd also refused to take the unnecessary ones issued as a routine standard to all ICU patients 'in case they were needed' for sleep, anxiety and other problems. The nurses supported her claim; I think they were enjoying the fight! But I was depressed, the opponents argued. Rosalind countered by telling them that I was bored out my skull because I had no mental challenge to keep my brain occupied. I would need special food, they then said. She told them that she'd been doing all my feeding, without any digestive problems or weight change, under the supervision of the dietician (who confirmed the statement) for the previous six weeks, while she'd been there for ten hours every day to train.

The meeting ended with a reluctant agreement to meet again one week later, after all the points had been considered. Diane decided that she would attend, on the grounds that she and Robert owned Action Mobility and could advise on equipment needs. There was no argument, so she sat across the circle from Rosalind to make eye contact. The opposition had been busy. They'd got a report from the physiotherapist to the effect that I was unable to move any muscles, so would be totally bedridden for the rest of my life, which would be a very short one. Rosalind pointed out that he'd never made an attempt to check my muscles and that, if he'd done his job properly, I'd still be able to get around as well as I had done, with a walker, before being admitted to hospital. But if I couldn't walk, I'd be trapped in the house. Diane produced a diagram of ramp her company would build at a day's notice. And how would I get upstairs to bed, now I was unable to be transferred to the stair lifts that were already installed? She produced a plan she'd drawn up to show how one corner of our living room, isolated from the dining and sitting areas by a screen, would become a hospital room with my bed, Rosalind's bed, plus space for equipment and storage in it. That was all very well, the opposition said, but I needed a ceiling lift to get me into or out of bed and it would take at least a month, or probably more, to have our ceiling strengthened and the lift installed. Diane produced a catalogue that contained a free-standing lift, ideal for the situation. As a last resort, they told us that hospital rules required us to have a support team of five people who would be prepared to perform suction on me in an emergency. Rosalind, forewarned, already had Danielle, our granddaughter with a nursing degree, plus four friends (Peter, Jill, Ann and Liz) signed up and they were scheduled to attend training sessions within the next few days. The day for my discharge (escape?) was to be in one week's time, on the following Wednesday.

But we hadn't quite finished. The next day, the doctor suddenly announced that the trach I'd had installed was too big, so he replaced it in a fairly painful procedure. On the Monday, Rosalind had to delay her arrival for the usual ten-hour day, because she had to stay home to supervise a team of cleaners hired to get the room ready for my return home. The doctor immediately decided that he'd made the wrong choice and needed to revert to the large trach after all and forced it in, with considerable difficulty. When she arrived to find me bleeding and the doctor off dealing with an emergency, she made her feelings known in an unmistakable manner. There were no more delaying tactics and I was duly packed off home by ambulance on the appointed day.

9   Change and Communication

We arrived home in the early afternoon of that Wednesday in May and I don't think I've ever felt more thankful for the pleasure of reaching any destination in my life. I can appreciate how a captured wild animal, or a prisoner who has been tortured, must feel on release from captivity. I'm being unfair, I know, after the care taken by the staff to keep me alive and healthy, but the narrow escape from permanent incarceration in a long-term facility haunted me for days (though we did send a token of thanks in the form of a large basket of fruit once the certainty of freedom had sunk in). My overwhelming feeling as the ambulance staff carried me into the house was gratitude for the haven of our peaceful home.

Not quite peaceful.

In the next three hours, a seemingly endless procession of people flowed through the house. Diane had supervised the process of getting the place set up for me and the whole living room around me was crammed with people, equipment and supplies that had been ordered by various sections of the health care system as being necessary for me. Rosalind was, understandably, overloaded with information. Every person who arrived needed to give her details about how the specific product or supply should be used. Most of the instructions were verbal and the ones that were more complex were contained in thick manuals. It was impossible for us to distinguish between vital items and those of useful, but not crucial, application. At the end of the barrage, the room was filled with food packages, wound dressing components, medications and a large selection of ointments or creams, as well as pieces of equipment designed to help Rosalind to keep me breathing, fed and able to be lifted around in the bed for washing, changing or dressing. By the end of the delivery process, we were exhausted.

If I had the chance to live my life over again, would I make the choice to have the same surgery performed? I've asked myself the same question many times and we've both discussed it frequently. The answer is that I honestly don't know. Probably I'd have chosen to go ahead with it, simply because it would have to be done eventually and it certainly removed a lot of anxiety, though the downside of being unable to speak (not applicable in all cases, incidentally) is definitely a major price to pay. Would I advise other people to make the same choice, then? Yes, if they have the excessive uncontrollable breathing problems that I had, with one possible exception.

At the suggestion of my respirologist, we'd decided to buy a Cough Assist machine. This is a device that pumps air, at a higher pressure than atmospheric level, deep into the lungs, then sucks it out again, along with any mucus accumulated there. Unfortunately it was very expensive and we'd delayed ordering one. We finally took the plunge, but delivery was not available for two months and I'd been forced to have the surgery before it arrived. I've used it ever since I got it and it clears out my mucus wonderfully. We both believe that, if it had arrived in time, the tracheotomy could have been delayed considerably.

There's another factor to be considered, though. The main reason for delay would have been to allow us to travel, now virtually impossible for me with a ventilator that needs recharging frequently. We would probably have gone to Britain again, under a false sense of security given by the ability of the Cough Assist to prevent mucus plugs, but it's a large, heavy machine that couldn't be taken on a flight. We'd also have been tempted to leave it at home on extended journeys by car and I could easily have suffered a fatal mucus plug on our travels when I wasn't regularly clearing out my lungs. One alternative, used in the days before Cough Assist equipment was available, is the Breath Stacker, a type of bellows operated manually, which would probably have worked in an emergency, though we've always found it less effective on the few occasions when we've tried it. In other words, delaying the tracheotomy might have been dangerous and, since I would probably have needed it six months later, it was perhaps a good move. The only real advantage, with no obvious possible drawbacks, of holding off would have been an extension of my ability to speak.

So we had to adapt in an extensive way to a major change in our circumstances. In theory, I was now unable to speak, bedridden instead of mobile, and could no longer eat or drink through my mouth.

This depressing state lasted for about 18 hours from the time I got home. The following morning, I insisted on getting dressed and leaving my bed. The wheelchair ordered for me hadn't arrived the previous day, as the suppliers had sent the wrong one in error ; they never actually brought the tilt chair until September and even then it was lacking important items that were supposed to be included. It was more than a year before I got a wheelchair that was, supposedly, complete and another eighteen months before it was fully functional. In the meantime, I still had the basic motor chair that Diane and Robert had found for me to use. I was hoisted into it and Rosalind rigged up an arrangement that allowed her to hang the ventilator from the handle and draped in a basket. I drove happily round the room a few times, then decided I would like to try standing. I managed it with the help of a few people and decided that I would refuse to accept the medical predictions of my future state of existence. In the following few weeks, we got a physiotherapist and a speech pathologist. The former expert managed to get me walking and I progressed, over the next few months, to the point where I could stagger across the living room, a distance of six metres, for six consecutive crossings. Sadly, she retired and her replacement was not happy to continue because of the risk of my falling. I'd realized that I was getting much more unsteady on my feet, so reluctantly abandoned any hopes of impending marathon participation.

The speech pathologist was also able to test my swallowing ability and told me that I shouldn't take anything by mouth but, if I wanted to live dangerously, I could try the experiment at my own risk, preferably with resuscitation equipment at hand. For some time, I managed to eat soft foods occasionally and still enjoy a drink of apple juice, but it's getting more difficult. I plan to stop when I reach the point where the entire contents of the juice container is poured down my chest instead of into my mouth. She worked, too, on the possibility of restoring my speaking ability but the effort was in vain; my tongue muscles were unable to function well enough for me to form words and all I could manage was an ape-like bellowing grunt, not at all suitable for polite conversation but giving us many laughs.

By this time, we'd realized that we had two major difficulties to overcome. The first, more critical, one was to avoid falling into depression. We were determined to maintain a positive attitude in the face of adversity and to achieve this aim by finding humour wherever we could. I think the success we achieved was thanks to my stubbornness ; certainly Rosalind has thanked and congratulated me many times on how I've managed to keep my spirits up, but I know I could never have done it without her constant and unfailing support. The method we adopted was to find something funny in everything that happened, as far as we possibly could. Every time I had a mishap, like stumbling, dropping something, or getting the wrong impression about what was said, we laughed. The same thing happened when Rosalind happened to make some small error in giving me food, or tried half a dozen times to understand what I wanted and performed several unwanted tasks before getting to the one I needed done. We were particularly amused by the fact that I was praised for achievements that would have been treated with embarrassment in earlier times. I was now complimented for the quality and quantity of the various solid, liquid or gaseous by-products excreted from my digestive or pulmonary systems. Every slight mishap, such as steering my chair into furniture (or too near somebody's feet!) or drooling down my shirt, was greeted with amusement. As a result, our home was filled with laughter and happiness.

The second big difficulty was the lack of any ability to communicate verbally on my part. Apparently I have, according to several people, a very expressive face (left over from years of experience as an actor!) and Rosalind became quite adept at guessing what I wanted, but there were times when she had to spend several minutes (again to our great amusement!) trying to interpret what I was saying. We had a letter card listing the alphabet, plus some symbols and a few useful words, that I could point to and get my request out fairly efficiently, but (though I moved too quickly at first) I eventually reached the point where a combination of poor muscle control and hand shakiness made spelling out messages too slow and inaccurate to be of much use.

Communication is a two-way process and I still get some amusement from the efforts of other people, mainly strangers or recent acquaintances, to make small talk with me. Close observation by these more intelligent members of the human species reveals that I am unable to breathe, speak, eat, or move without the aid of complex machines. Thus, any fool knows at a glance that I am also dim-witted and completely deaf, so must be addressed in a particular way. The correct procedure is to place their face six inches directly in front of mine, bending to get close enough, then shout loudly, speaking very slowly, with exaggerated mouth movement, restricting vocabulary to simple words suitable for talking to a baby. If they can harness a good supply of saliva to increase the sensation of intimacy by spraying the odd few drops of spittle into my face, the conversation takes on a much more desirable atmosphere of personal satisfaction for them.

My response is to relax my facial muscles and turn my head slightly to one side, allowing the lower jaw to drop and a stream of drool to escape down my chin. At the same time I move my tongue so that lip-reading indicates that, if I could speak, I would be uttering the words "Goo! Goo! Mmm! Wah! Dah!" several times. This elicits the delighted, enthusiastic, laughing remark of "Oh, look at him! See! He can understand what I say to him!" Rosalind, embarrassed, used to tell me off roundly as soon as we were in private before we both burst out laughing. We now skip the intermediate step and proceed directly to the laughter.

If people feel the need to demonstrate more affection, there are two standard techniques. The milder one is to stroke my hair, pat me on the head, or clutch my hand, back, shoulder, etc. If these are inadequate to express their emotion, they (generally older ladies with a tendency to slight excess of weight, symptoms of impending senility, and unsteadiness in walking) plant what they mistakenly assume to be a fond kiss on my cheek. It's actually a wet slobber, containing remnants of their last two or three meals and leaves a slimy smear of nasty goo, further contaminated by lumps of greasy lipstick, on my face. I have no defence. I can't even raise a surreptitious hand high enough to wipe the filth off, so I have to wait for Rosalind to take pity on me.

Well, fellow ALS patients, you will realize that you can give such well-meaning people some idea of how to improve immensely the quality of life for their severely handicapped friends. Show this to them if you want to avoid the same experience. I'm sure they will really appreciate the effort you have made to create a more meaningful relationship between you.

At the stage I had reached by this time, we tried other methods. I could still type on my computer, so I had a means of getting messages out. When touching the keys became too difficult because of lost arm mobility, I was able to get a mouse-controlled onscreen keyboard (which I'm still using to type any documents, including this book) that allowed me to keep on communicating, but I wasn't too happy with the limited communication process. The next step was to get a speaking machine that made it possible for me to type words on a screen and press a key to have them spoken. I'm currently working on the latest version, which allows me to gaze at letters, words, symbols, etc. on a screen and blink at the correct moment to select the one I want. It's a very slow process that doesn't really let me take part in a conversation, because the topic has moved on by the time I've typed and spoken my contribution, though our friends do get a lot of amusement by trying to work out which bit of the conversation I'm referring to. Its main useful feature is that it allows me to prepare remarks to present on a future occasion. I've done this for telephone interviews or conversations and have even used it to present a few guest lectures in a university course. My speaking device has also had one invaluable accessory installed; the machine is fitted with means of controlling the TV by blinking. Rosalind is delighted not to have to struggle with the task of trying to understand what I want to watch while she needs to leave me parked in front of the set when she has work that needs her attention!

10   Sources of help

The main purpose of this chapter is to give advice to newly-diagnosed ALS patients about how and where they can seek useful information or assistance in their efforts to cope with the conditions under which they're forced to live by the illness. The content is derived from my own experiences over the past several years and may not be totally applicable to everybody, but I believe many parts will be relevant to most patients and caregivers.

The first source to consider is your own intelligence. Human brains are far more powerful than we've believed in the past and have an immense ability to control the body or invent useful aids to improve life. The first question that you should ask your own brain is whether you want to live with all the problems you'll have to face or would prefer to die as soon as possible. Both are valid attitudes and there are many factors, such as financial hardship, the effects on those around you, or your views on the quality of life. If you choose the latter option, I firmly believe that your brain will almost certainly help you by shutting down bodily functions. We've all heard of many people who, after losing the will to live, have died quickly. Indeed, I've known or heard of half a dozen people who felt that way and all of them did just that. My wish for you, if you're in this category, is that you may not suffer too much before your wish is granted (but I also hope that you're a fast reader to give you time to finish this book and see what those making the alternative choice will encounter!).

If you prefer to extend life for as long as possible, there are three approaches that I've come across. Some people get very angry, ranting at God, or their genes, or the world, or life in general, etc. Others become resigned but unhappy, constantly dwelling on questions of *why me?* And broadcasting their misery widely in print or vocal versions. Both of these reactions, to my mind, are a complete waste of energy and time that could be put to far better use. The third group of people try as I do, to accept the situation and rise above it. If you belong to this category, then I'm convinced that your mind will help you by finding the willpower to fight against early death. Positive attitude has been shown many times to bring about results that were thought unlikely or impossible.

You can also use your head to find activities that interest you. Reading, writing, following a sport, studying a language, exploring the history of a bygone era and similar occupations will give your mind something to focus on, deflecting your thoughts from any depressing dwelling on your situation. The other way you can keep your brain active is to make life more pleasant by inventing new ways of doing things. Rosalind and I, between us, have introduced these ideas : use of a sock to cover the sharp edges of my G-tube, which formerly scratched my abdomen and caused a rash ; placing a carpentry mask with a folded paper towel or handkerchief inside it to absorb large amounts of drool I produce when I put my head down to read or type ; drinking from the spout of a Nettipot (originally intended for pouring saline solution into the sinuses) instead of a glass that poured liquid down my face ; using powdered Bentonite clay mixed with water or tea tree oil to cure thrush on my tongue or a fungal infection near my G-tube site.

Your own intelligence should also be used to examine advice given to you by other people. Well-meaning friends told us that we should move house, when I was first diagnosed, into a bungalow, an apartment, or a seniors' residence. We resisted all the suggestions, because we wanted to stay in the neighbourhood where we'd lived and made friends for forty years, and because we could think of nothing worse than being surrounded by old people with old minds. The only potential benefit of a move would be to reduce Rosalind's workload in the house or garden, but we could achieve that by hiring help at a far lower cost (and with much less stress!) than a move. We've never once regretted that decision.

The other advice you should examine critically is medical opinion. Remember that you know your own body far better than any doctor does. Remember, too, that ALS is not the usual kind of medical case that can be slotted into a standard set of rules that can be applied to predict how the illness will progress. Doctors love to base a prognosis on the established statistical evidence gleaned from other patients, but this simply doesn't work for ALS. The symptoms are so variable in each individual case that nobody can ever guess which part of the body will be affected and when, or how fast, deterioration will happen. Hence, you should take pronouncements by a doctor as a mere expression of opinion, not necessarily a correct forecast of what's inevitably going to happen to you, then think carefully about how accurate the opinion might be.

Having said that, I must emphasize that I am not recommending that you ignore completely every piece of medical advice offered to you, just to consider it carefully before adopting it. You will need information on where the best advice can be found and there are useful sources you can check. Your family doctor, the local hospital staff, government officials, a phone directory, friends, a minister of religion and other possible places can be consulted and should lead to the goal you want. A couple of decades ago, I'd have included books in my list of helpful sources but, in these modern times, the Internet is far more likely to be consulted, since its information is, in general, more up to date. The same precautions regarding critical examination should be followed, though. I've seen lots of rubbish there, posted by idiots who have no clue what they're talking about.

The help of family and friends should also be sought and we have been very lucky in this respect. Diane, our eldest daughter, plus her husband, Robert and their daughter, Madeleine, offered to move in with us when it became obvious that the task of taking care of me would be too difficult for Rosalind if she also had to deal with her own household tasks, as well as those I'd always done. The arrangement works superbly for all of us. Diane does all the shopping and cooking, while Robert looks after maintenance and helps to keep the garden in order. Madeleine, now aged 12, is a delight to have around and it has given us so much pleasure to watch her growing up. Even her dog, Merlin, has valiantly carried out his duties as occasional garden soil fertilizer!

Amazingly, given the strong personalities of all our family members, the arrangement has worked extremely well, with no fights or disagreements of any kind. Rosalind's food appears in front of her and Diane makes sure that meals are there for her at the weekend, when the three of them go to their own place. Their home is well over an hour away and Action Mobility, the business they own, is a ten-minute drive from our house, so living with us does provide this small benefit for them. Our other two daughters, Hilary and Keirsten, live too far away (in Wales in the latter case) to be able to help in the same way, but phone calls and visits as often as possible let us know of their strong support.

We have many friends, some of them longstanding and others new (including several who, we previously thought, didn't want to know us!), too numerous, in general, to mention by name. Suffice it to say that they have brought joy into our lives and given us plenty of opportunities for laughter. Of special note are the ones who agreed to be on my support team in my escape from hospital, Ann, Peter, Jill and Liz, who have all continued to provide us with tremendous help. When I was first diagnosed, Ann phoned within a couple of days and offered to give me exercises regularly. She is trained in the area, was a leader in exercise classes at the university when I was similarly involved, and is now a staff member and personal trainer at the

YMCA/YWCA, so I accepted the offer with alacrity! She has given me exercises tailored to challenge my muscles to the limit, while gradually taking into account their steadily declining ability, every week for almost seven years now.

At about the same time, Peter and Jill asked if we would let them be our liaison with church when we couldn't be really involved there. Again, we accepted gratefully and enjoy weekly visits from them to keep us up to date and share many laughs about life in general. Jill is a skilled seamstress and has modified many of my garments to make it possible for me to wear them. We also see Liz every week and, as she was a friend from our theatre days, she keeps us well informed about events there. She also readily does errands when Rosalind needs anything special buying and has made warm articles of unusual clothing that are vital for my winter comfort.

The usual problem facing a new ALS patient is the financial burden that lies ahead. The costs of treatment are extremely high and, if you make the choice (as we did) to have home care, then the expense will be transferred from the hospital to you. Even if you have health insurance, there will be many purchases, for equipment, supplies, transport by mobility taxi, stair lift and ramp, etc., that have to be met from your own pockets. So you need to find sources of money that you can tap.

In Canada, the ALS Society has limited funds to support needy patients, especially after the incredibly successful ice bucket challenge. However, the society tends to apply a means test to all applicants and we were classed as too wealthy (I never knew there was such a thing!) to qualify. CCAC is an umbrella organization that gives us tremendous support in providing care staff and supplies like dressings, trach accessories, etc. Government sources, under provincial jurisdiction in Canada, are generally not prepared to provide money as such, but provide me with funding to support the cost of specific needs and will always subsidize equipment purchases if the right hoops are traversed. The most familiar source of this category is ADP, the Assistive Devices Programme and most equipment suppliers have access to it, giving them the means to access it on your behalf. My wheelchair was 75% funded from this source, with the remainder coming from my insurance, though I think I could have got help from other places if the need had arisen. Another similar organization is the CEP, or Central Equipment Pool, where necessary items are available for loan, sometimes without charge and sometimes at a fee representing a small proportion of the actual cost of the machine. My ventilator and suction device, both of them essential for my survival, are on loan without charge, while my speaking machine, not absolutely necessary but a very important luxury, is provided if I pay a substantial annual fee (not covered by insurance).

There are two more sources of help that I need to mention. The first is Rosalind, who has given me the inspiration and support that have continually kept up my spirits with her unfailing devotion in difficult times. I couldn't possibly have been able to cope with the illness so well without her. The second is the religious faith that we both share, stemming from the beliefs that were given to us from childhood by our families. They have provided us with a solid foundation on which to stand. There are, too, several categories of people who have shared their special skills with us, the health care workers meeting so many of my needs, but I think they deserve a chapter to themselves, the next one of this book.

11   Health care professionals

One group of people I depend on so heavily, those involved in taking care of my well-being, are so vital that I would say with confidence that I couldn't have survived without their help, either in dealing with medical problems or in preventing them from arising by keeping me clean.

The most qualified and senior members are the doctors, some of whom I've already mentioned. Apart from our opponent-cum-respecter during the two months I was in hospital, the urologist who almost killed me and the neurologist who first diagnosed ALS, we've met only a couple of dubious ones, both of them being in the Emergency Departments of the hospital when I had to go there with breathing problems. One of them mistook my ventilator for an oxygen supply container and was quite put out when we finally managed to correct her mistake, claiming that she'd never seen or heard of a ventilator. The other was similarly uninformed, but clued in a bit more quickly. One more example is worth noting. When I first had the G-tube inserted, we were unaware that it had to be changed from time to time and only found out when the plastic tube on it began to decompose. The problem was soon resolved by a doctor who voluntarily gave up his lunch hour to replace it. We made sure of getting the second change done in good time, but a major issue arose a few days later. I was unable to keep any food, or even water, in my body, but suffered from nausea and diarrhoea. I went to

Emergency, where I was crammed full of Gravol and sent home, supposedly cured, five days later. Within two days, I was back there with worse symptoms and the doctor decided on a colonoscopy. I was only semi-conscious, but Rosalind, who had been telling him that she felt there was some connection with the G-tube change, finally persuaded him to recheck all the other test results first. She was right. He discovered that, when the G-tube had originally been inserted, almost two years earlier, it had been passed through my colon instead of directly into my stomach. In the first change it had followed the same route but, in the recent second one, the tube had deviated so that all the food and water was delivered directly into my colon and hence expelled within twenty minutes.

In all other cases, the doctors I've needed have been excellent. Our family doctor immediately volunteered to make home visits once he heard the diagnosis. My dermatologist offered to come to the house, bringing liquid nitrogen to burn off precancerous lesions which my skin develops from time to time. Our dentist has been here twice (and refused to take any pay) and arranged for a hygienist to treat me at home as long as no fillings are necessary. The surgeons who put me back together when various bits had stopped working performed operations outside their working hours. Less exalted specialists have also agreed to treat me at home. They include a chiropodist, a physiotherapist and a hair stylist and their willingness to provide home services makes life so much more convenient and pleasant for us. We are truly fortunate and grateful.

Nurses, too, have gone out of their way to support me. The ones in the hospital were always willing to do extra work in a cheerful manner to enhance my comfort or provide me with more help in the form of exercise, reaching things, or changing TV channels, etc. Since my return home, nurses have fallen into two categories, daily and respite ones. Every day, I'm examined to check that vital signs (blood pressure, pulse, breathing, oxygen saturation, skin condition, water retention and the various excretions required for healthy survival) are all in the correct condition. The nurse then changes the dressings on my trach and G-tube sites, treating infections and any other problems encountered. Respite nurses are those who spend several hours taking care of me while Rosalind goes out for a well-earned break to see friends, visit the gym, go to shops (usually seeking items needed for my care!), have tea, or do anything else that she fancies. Both groups of nurses, over the past years, have become good friends and provided us with the pleasure of their company and plenty of laughter.

We have the same kind of relationship with my psw (personal support workers). As far as we're concerned, these people are the main backbone of the health care system. They work for little more than the minimum wage, putting in many hours of hard work in an effort to make a reasonable income, but are treated abysmally, with little or no respect, by the agencies employing them. They are often called at a few hours' notice and expected to rush to the client's home, which may be a twenty-minute drive away, without being given any travel time. On other occasions, their shift may be arbitrarily cancelled so that they have an hour in the early morning, with another two or three scattered through the afternoon and until late evening, making it impossible for them to do anything else during the day.

Their abilities vary. Some of them, like our primary psw, are superb. On numerous occasions, when the agency has been unable to find anyone to fill a shift, he has stepped in, even on his day off or at a difficult time, to make sure that my needs are met. He is extremely competent and conscientious, as are several others who come, but we have had some who are virtually useless. Rosalind soon has them removed from my roster with a quick phone call! The agency unhesitatingly takes her word that they simply can't carry out their task, which necessarily ranges from hurling me round like a sack of beetroots (more stylish and high-class, I feel, than potatoes!) to gently caressing various intimate (and unmentionable) regions of the anatomy. A couple of the ones who still come seem to be training for a career in proctology or gelding, and one lady apparently believes that electric shavers are only effective if applied from behind the skin. I suspect that my face would be marginally less damaged if she used a grindstone. I tolerate all the indignities and discomfort heaped on me with patient acceptance, because the alternative is not very pleasant to contemplate! I've decided that I will do all I possibly can, little though it is, to help and avoid, again as far as possible, doing anything that could hinder their work. I sometimes hear of patients they encounter with exactly the opposite attitude and their feelings about such people are, understandably, a little negative.

I get pleasure from the stories some of the psw tell, because we meet people from many parts of the world, some of them refugees who have lived through horrendous experiences. I have to admit, though, that I get quite a bit of amusement from the way that psw operate. Because the work load is heavy, two of them are allocated to my morning care. The first one sets up the table holding the wash equipment in a convenient place beside the bed, then the second one arrives and moves it to the bottom of the bed. The first one, returning with a bowl of water, moves it almost back to its first position, then the other psw moves it towards the second place. The oscillation continues for perhaps three or four more cycles, with the distance travelled decreasing gradually, until the table ends up in a location that's not particularly convenient for either psw but not so inconvenient that any protest is valid. If the two are relatively new to working with me, they give me enjoyment when I hear them trying to establish dominance by advising each other how a particular task should be done, especially if both are wrong.

Then comes the polite discussion of which position each will take. When I am getting a wash, I lie on my right side for the process of cleaning up the nether (and messy) regions of my body. The two psw will then engage in gentle debate about who should stand on the right, or pee-side, and the left, or poo-side, of my body. The conversation proceeds along the lines of "why don't you go on his left" if dominance is established or "shall I take the left side?" if one of the two is in the mood for altruism or martyrdom. My supreme moment of pleasure eventually arrives as the left-hand worker, busily scraping the mess away, stretches the nearby muscles so far that the local orifice opens too widely and must then recoil and stagger backwards from the unexpected, but inevitable, rapid expulsion of gas. Fun is there for the asking in the most unlikely places if you choose to look for it!

12   Bureaucracy

Of the various negative aspects of the life thrust on to us, the worst by far is the bureaucracy we are forced to deal with. The only explanation for it that makes sense is that the health system is heavily overloaded with small-minded people who have very little real power but use what bit they do have to obstruct and frustrate the wishes of other people, who have to depend on their services to live as normal a life as possible.

The reason is fairly simple to identify and lies in the vast overload of non-productive management that permeates the whole system. The people occupying these positions fall generally into two categories. The first of them consists of former nurses, 'promoted' (usually with the loss of a good nurse from the ranks of practitioners) from within the ranks of the profession to work in a supervisory capacity. They each oversee the work of several other nurses providing services to sick people in the community, giving advice or help when the need arises. The other group's duties are focused on the task of controlling the financial aspects of health care to make sure that the budget constraints are not exceeded. Unfortunately, there are many negative aspects to both types of job. The employees in them tend to spend far too much of their working day sitting in a cubicle in a room with a few dozen other people, all entering data into a computer. The former nurses, overwhelmed by the task, are seldom needed for practical nursing applications and slowly lose the skills instilled into them during training.

The financial people become fixated on reducing costs to the point where necessary expenditures are denied. They have no training in the nursing field, so are incapable of distinguishing between vital and unimportant end-uses of the supplies requested.

This preponderance of pen-pushing (or key-tapping, in this modern computer age) minions, sadly, is not restricted to a single layer of management. Each member of one level is under the supervision of someone else in a higher position of authority, with the task of overseeing the activities of several groups of people at the lower level and must report in turn to a supervisor at an even higher level. The higher the level of management, naturally, the greater the salary, so each person in the system is constantly striving to do a better job, translated into a more impressive set of paperwork and the frustration of not getting promotion reduces any tendency towards generosity in the majority left at the lower rank.

And that, basically, is the root of major problems in the health system. The overall budget is fixed and the aim is to avoid exceeding it. The people best skilled in this ability are the financial, rather than nursing, members of the staff, so the proportion of medically-trained employees diminishes as higher levels of authority are reached. Three negative results follow. First, the medical facilities, staff, supplies, etc. are controlled by people with no ability to distinguish between necessary and merely useful requests. Second, the high salaries commanded by these people mean that less money is available to pay the hands-on workers, like nurses or psw, who actually care for the patients, with a resulting shortage of staff and medical needs, causing wards to be left vacant, longer delays in getting surgery and overstretched caregivers. The third, arguably most serious, result is the fact that the cost of providing health care becomes the most important factor to be considered. All the facilities and agencies in the system proudly declare that the patient is Number One in their priority list, but this is clearly not the case. The almighty dollar invariably outranks every other consideration and prevents much of the potentially excellent care from taking place.

Now, how does this affect me personally? I should state right from the start that, in comparison with other patients I have met or heard about, I'm very fortunate. This is partly because ALS is known to be an illness with critical needs, but mostly from Rosalind's ceaseless efforts to challenge the system until she either gets what I need or is satisfied that what she has achieved is the best available. As a result, I get excellent treatment from all my nurses and psw, with virtually every need and wish granted. These helpers are supplied by an agency, as are the various supplies, such as medical dressings or creams, syringes, and other necessary items. In one of the multiple levels of management, there is a position entitled case manager, a person supervising the agencies and the way in which caregivers or supplies are provided for me. Their effectiveness ranges widely, but the two who have been responsible for my welfare are excellent. If we have the slightest problem that doesn't get rectified quickly. Rosalind only has to phone them for a solution to be found as if by magic. Thanks to their efforts and Rosalind's vigilant persistence, the number of problems has declined drastically, so we rarely have to call on them for help at present.

However, frustrations still exist as a consequence of the pervasive bureaucracy. We are only allowed to order supplies once every two weeks, on a fixed day and before a specific time, for collection from a central distribution site the following week. The order form must be filled out by a nurse, who must then submit it to an office to be checked. From there, it goes to another office for approval, after which it is sent to yet another office at the supply company for passing to their store workers, who prepare and pack the listed supplies. Errors can occur at any of these stages and correcting them is a long process requiring vast amounts of time and paperwork. There is a defined quota for each item and, if it has to be exceeded for medical reasons, the process can take up to four months and the intervention of the case manager. The situation becomes even worse if the item is not listed in the official manual used to define legitimate supplies. In the midst of our frustrations, we narrowly avoid a descent into insanity by amusing ourselves with predictions of the mistakes or delays in the order each fortnight.

Another example of the effects of officialdom on our life has been the situation arising when I needed minor changes made to my wheelchair. This has happened several times and there was invariably a lengthy wait to be endured. The worst one happened when I needed modifications to the control console because the mobility of my hand was declining to the point where I found driving very difficult. I was forced to have the changes made by the original supplier because of the ADP monopoly legislation and it took fifteen months, with half a dozen phone calls, before the job was done. It would have taken even longer, I believe, if I hadn't written a strongly-worded letter to the ADP, with copies to our local MP, the suppliers and a few newspapers!

Somehow, we have managed to find sources of amusement, usually by regaling friends with the continuing saga of mishaps, in all these adversities, but it has been no simple task. In fact, it was easier to cope with the tribulations of ALS than to deal with the obstructions of bureaucracy. We laughed at both, but the laughter was perhaps slightly more sardonic when it was caused by coping with the system!

13   The current situation

To give newly-diagnosed ALS patients some idea of how the illness progresses, I want to describe my present condition and how I deal with the various changes I have to go through. In this way, they can have advance warning of what they must face in the future.

So, about seven years after the symptoms first began to be evident, I have reached the stage where I can't breathe, speak, eat, or move any part of my body without considerable help from machines and other people. I still have a small amount of mobility in my arms and fingers, allowing me to type when Rosalind sets up my computer in exactly the right place. I'm completely bowel incontinent and partly bladder incontinent, in that I can use a urinal but have a lot of leakage between uses. I estimate that up to 400 mL escape the urinal daily in this way, particularly at night. I still have full nerve sensation of touch, temperature, or pain, but not any indication of bowel action needs or occurrence. As Rosalind puts it, I don't notice food going in and I don't notice the digestive end-product going out.

I become fatigued very quickly, to the point where I can't do anything slightly strenuous, such as typing, for more than about an hour without feeling exhausted. My thermal regulation is also very poor. At times, my body can feel so hot that I'm concerned about fainting, then, in literally less than ten minutes, I begin an uncontrollable fit of shivering from being too cold. This experience is, of course, simulated in the well-known Ice Bucket Challenge, a fundraising activity that swept the world recently and was enthusiastically supported by all my family, including poor Merlin, a bemused little dog. When I'm turned on one side during the clean-up process, I have great difficulty in breathing and often have to take a break. I try to find a time when the pause doesn't lead to the creation of an unholy mess on the bedding, with a gesture of apology hiding a well-concealed grin from sight when I'm unsuccessful! I also drool a lot, especially when I have my head down, as in typing or reading. My facial muscles don't function too well so, when I try to smile, I resemble the village idiot, as you will notice in the front cover photo of the book. I take a few non-prescription medicines, including the usual vitamins, collodal silver to remove toxins and hydrogen peroxide as a lung cleanser (I have the clearest lungs they've ever seen in an ALS patient at the local hospital, I'm told).

What I have left, though, is important. My brain is still functioning as well as it ever did and is probably in an improved state, since it has very few distractions to deal with. My sight and hearing are both in excellent condition, though I now need a cheap pair of non-prescription glasses for reading and an annual ear syringing to hear quiet music or conversation. I can still make small movements of my arms, allowing me to type when Rosalind sets up my computer, but I can detect small losses in this ability on almost a daily basis.

In Chapter 10, I list the various ways in which people with ALS respond to their diagnosis, by ranting, self-pitying, or practising placid martyrdom. I think my approach avoids the pitfalls existing in each of these reactions. I have chosen, in a phrase coined by Rosalind, to **embrace** the illness. That is, I accept it as a normal part of life, to be tolerated and dealt with in the same way as any other inconvenience. There's no point in getting angry, or bemoaning my misfortune, or becoming a martyr, because none of these reactions will do the slightest bit of good in curing the condition and will actually lower the quality of life by forcing the mind to dwell excessively on the situation. The best thing to do, I believe, is to ignore or forget that I have the problem and get on with my life as well as possible, given the restrictions placed on me by its presence. In other words, I adopt a modified lifestyle and get as much enjoyment as possible while I follow it. Instead of regretting what I have lost, I focus on what I still have and enjoy it as much as I can.

I have a routine that has to be followed seven days a week. It includes the obvious features, like feeding, cleaning and dressing or undressing, with some extra activities thrown in to avoid boredom. I type for an hour before my day begins while my breakfast is passed into my stomach, using a feed bag suspended from an IV pole to drip it in via the G-tube as I sit up in bed, then for a further one or two one-hour sessions during the day. I stretch extensively every muscle in my body when I awaken and perform a series of limited exercises daily, with eight types ranging from about three to thirty minutes' time, working on different sets of muscles, to keep my body in as good a shape as possible. I get the rest of my liquid diet (no, not that kind!) fed at a faster rate by a syringe twice more, at lunch time and in the early evening. There are three daily visits from psw, involving two of them immediately after breakfast and one each in the afternoon and at bedtime. A nurse comes once a day to change the dressings on my trach and G-tube sites, together with a quick check of my vital signs. I enjoy trading jokes, with the psw and nurse, about such topics as my declining state of health or insistence on having their work done absolutely exactly and properly. At the end of the day, after the last psw has gone, we watch TV for an hour, then Rosalind does a cough assist before settling me with exchanged words of love and a few laughs.

This daily sequence is occasionally broken. A physiotherapist visits once a week to do range-of-motion exercises and our friend, Ann, arrives on another day to give me an hour of different ones. There are other distractions from routine, too, almost always with a need to rearrange one or more of the scheduled events of feed, psw or nurse times. We have medical appointments to keep, go for walks or shopping trips and try to get to church each Sunday (though this is a fifty-minute walk each way, so depends on weather conditions and psw efficiency). We walk whenever possible, partly because mobility taxis are often late but mainly because they also make me ill with motion sickness. As a result, I tend to be stuck at home for the four months of winter each year, though I can get into our sun room by going out through the front door, down the ramp and back indoors through the garage if there is little or no snow on the ground.

Despite all these drawbacks to a normal life, Rosalind and I both agree that we have never been happier in our lives than we are now (though we have, of course, been as happy on many occasions). I think the reason is that most of the stress of coping with life has disappeared. Rosalind has always hated flying, but we no longer can do, despite our former love of travel to see family members and visit other countries. Conversely, we have a ready excuse for declining invitations to places we don't want to visit. We never need to worry about what health problems might hit us, because we've already coped with a pretty nasty one and proved to ourselves that we can rise above adversity by treating it with a stubborn sense of humour. So our house is filled with laughter and happiness.

Does this mean that I'm glad I contracted ALS? No, of course not; what a stupid question! There are so many things I miss but, with determination, I can find compensating mechanisms. Of all I've lost, I think the gift of speech is the one that has hit me hardest. Using a letter board or speaking machine allows me to 'speak' to people, but these subsitutes are so slow that real conversation simply doesn't happen. Instead, we amuse ourselves by having a laugh about my efforts to get what I want to say across by miming and mouthing words, or at the attempts of Rosalind and the psw to understand what I mean. My second most difficult loss is the ability to eat. I used to love my food and now have to survive on a tasteless sludge that insists on leaving a nasty flavour in my mouth. I am resigned to the situation, but I always ask Rosalind to tell me what she's eating and conjuring up memories of its taste. Occasionally, when time and weather permit, we go out for a meal, either by ourselves or with a few family members or friends.

Next on my list of lost pleasures is the ability to travel. I've visited over 100 countries in my life and organized a score of tours for family, friends or students and really enjoyed using the languages I can understand. I miss this, but I have books, TV shows and friends who describe their travels or recall the pleasure I gave them on the foreign holidays I organized for them. Again, I use my memories to relive happy times. The only negative part of life that I can't easily deal with is the mental anguish I suffer when I watch Rosalind struggle to carry out tasks, especially banking or other paperwork and gardening, which used to be my responsibility.

There are, too, plenty of other compensations. We enjoy a stream of visitors, who all seem to like coming to see us. They are kind enough to say that we are amazing and an inspiration to them, heaping praise or admiration on us for the way we're dealing with a situation they claim would be difficult or impossible for them to live with. We discourage excessive adulation on the grounds that it might give us swollen heads and absolutely forbid any hint of pity or sympathy. Anybody trying to offer these, or any other negative feelings, is politely, but firmly, dissuaded. I've met so many wonderful people who would never have become friends if I'd stayed healthy. Strangers rush to help us by little (to them!) acts, such as opening doors or helping Rosalind to remove or put on my coat, which are a struggle for her. Our nurses and psw tell us that they love their visits to our house (including the classical music playing throughout the time they're here!) and that there is competition for what many of them regard as more of a social event despite the hard work involved. Another benefit is that I've been able to do a tremendous amount of writing that I couldn't possibly have managed without all the enforced time on my hands given to me by ALS. In short, the means of finding happiness in what could be a devastating time are there if you choose to look for them.

A particularly unexpected benefit is the way in which honours have been bestowed on us, none of which would have happened if I'd never had the illness. When the ALS finally brought to an end our long association with the local theatre, as actors, directors, technical workers and Board members, the group honoured us by granting us life membership and naming the theatre foyer The Slater Room, with a plaque and our photograph mounted on the wall. The following year, the mayor, who had seen a report of the event, gave us jointly the award of citizens of the year for our contribution to the Arts. Then the students of the 1971 graduating class, of which I was Honorary President, established a substantial annual scholarship in our names. Finally, Rosalind received a Hero in the Home award from the regional health authority, a well-deserved tribute to her dedication in looking after me.

Most crucial to my survival, indeed, is the tremendous and total support given unselfishly to me by Rosalind. She promised, when the illness was diagnosed seven years ago, that she would dedicate her life to my care and she has kept her word without fault. There has never been a single occasion when she has failed to give me anything I needed, whether physical support or advocacy in the face of obstruction from officialdom. Of one thing I am certain; I'm extremely relieved that our roles aren't reversed, because, unlike me, she loves to talk incessantly (I tell her she has a major problem, in that people won't stop listening to her) and the enforced inability to speak would drive her insane. She claims that she couldn't have been as stoic as me in the way I've handled the situation, but I know that I could never take care of her anywhere nearly as well as she has cherished me. She has even offered, when I have had enough of living as a vegetable, to help me to die, but I don't think I'll ever accept the offer; I love her too much to condemn her to potential prosecution for an illegal action.

14   A glimpse of the future

Well, I seem to have completed the book. If you learn nothing else from it, remember the two most important actions you must take if you truly want to find happiness in the dark place that is ALS. First, find a goal to focus on to the exclusion of worry about your illness. Second, look for something you can laugh about in every situation you encounter.

My own next goal, now the book is finished, is an obvious one, because I think I may still have a bit of typing ability left in my muscles. I hope so, because I have two more plays buzzing around inside my head, one bursting to get out and the other still just a glimmer of an idea. Apart from them, what else do I see in the offing? There are two distinct aspects of this topic, my own personal future and that of ALS in general.

In the first of these subjects, I'm firmly convinced that I will eventually die. Death is inevitable and I really don't see any genuine possibility of getting round that obstacle to eternal life. There again, I'm comforted by the knowledge that you'll be sharing the same destiny, whether or not you also share the same illness. (It could happen sooner than we expect, given our current determination to destroy our planet and everybody in it!). One interesting possibility occurs to me. If the religious faith that has sustained me throughout all the adversities of life, especially during the past seven years, is to fulfil its promise, I'll be going to a joyful afterlife when my time on earth ends. There, according to science, the time dimension is non-existent, allowing me to move forwards and backwards at will and meet relatives or friends from my past. Combining the two doctrines leads to one possible hypothesis, that I am already dead and happily in contact with the friends and family members who have predeceased me or aren't yet born. Perhaps, because I already dream about some of them, I should seriously consider the idea as a valid one! If it is, then death becomes just a matter of a simple transition from one state to another, a sort of promotion to the Premier League. The principle makes the thought of death much less terrifying, though I must confess that I'm not greatly looking forward to the potentially unpleasant preliminary process of reaching that state.

As far as ALS in general is concerned, I'm totally confident that a complete cure will be found within the next 5 (or 10 or 20 or 50!) years. It will take place in three stages, I believe. The first will be the discovery of a drug that will slow down the rate of deterioration of the body of people living with the illness. Next will come a drug that halts completely any such degradation. The final step will be a process by which the harmful changes will be reversed. (Depending on the effectiveness of this latter treatment, it may also be necessary to develop a vaccine to eliminate the onset of the affliction in the first case).

Now, how will this sequence affect me personally? Research into the first step is already taking place, but the only widely available drug, Rilutek, has not been unequivocally shown to be effective. It's said to lengthen life by a short time, if at all, and is likely to introduce a real risk of liver, or other organ, damage. Any replacement substance must avoid these drawbacks. The second stage, which could evolve rapidly from the discoveries encountered in the first one, has to be subjected to the same conditions. For reversal of changes, there are only two approaches that are feasible at present. The first is to fool the brain into producing a fresh supply of motor neurons and the second is to find them from an external source for insertion into the body. Both methods, presumably, may need topping up treatments, since there's a strong possibility that the immune system could destroy motor neurons in the same way that it did to cause ALS in the first place. In addition, an external supply is currently only obtainable from stem cells, an area of research strongly discouraged on legal and ethical grounds in today's world.

So I must ask myself if any of these avenues of approach would be feasible in my case. I suspect that the first two might not be of much use to me because, once deterioration has gone as far as mine, slowing down or stopping its rate of progress would scarcely be noticeable. The only reasonable exception would be the case of a treatment that prevented the loss of hand mobility, stopping me from typing, without causing liver or other organ damage.

The third technique, now, is of far more interest, though I don't deceive myself into believing that it would provide an instant cure for me. Even if such a miracle as replenishment of motor neurons happened tomorrow, it wouldn't magically solve my problems. It's true that my exercises have kept my muscles from becoming completely atrophied, but I don't do them in the vain hope of throwing off the illness. It takes about two years for a baby to be able to walk and I would expect to need at least the same amount of time for me to be transformed from a near-vegetable to a fully functioning and independent human being. I would expect that the large muscles operating the limbs would recover first, because they're easier to exercise. I'd then face the difficult task of persuading the rest of my body to follow suit. The muscles operating my digestive system, including bowel control, can't readily be exercised, nor can those responsible for stopping incontinence. I think, though, that the breathing mechanism may be the most difficult to restore, mainly because it's so crucial for survival and it would be unable to find a substitute solution in the event of failure.

Would I be willing to join a medical trial of any treatment taking place for this potential 'cure' if one become available? I think I probably would, but my decision would depend on the details of the procedure. If it necessitated going to a distant location for regular appointments, for example, I'd be far less prepared to take part than I would if it merely involved attending once or twice at the local hospital. At present, of course, there's no need for me to make the decision, since such a trial isn't yet being considered.

Thus, I have no choice other than to continue plodding along, thanks to Rosalind's constant care and support, until I eventually reach Heaven, or whatever name is used to identify the place of a happy afterlife. I sincerely hope they will accept jokers there!

WORK PUBLISHED BY KEITH SLATER

Non-fiction

The Thermal Behaviour of Textiles, Textile Institute, 1976.
Comfort Properties of Textiles, Textile Institute, 1977.
Textile Mechanics, Vol. 1, Textile Institute, 1977.
Directing Amateur Theatre, Charles C. Thomas, 1984.
Human Comfort, Charles C. Thomas, 1985.
Textile Mechanics, Vol. 2, Textile Institute, 1986.
Textile Mechanics, Vol. 3, Textile Institute, 1986.
Yarn Evenness, Textile Institute, 1986.
Textile Degradation, Textile Institute, 1991.
The Social Costs of Human Progress, Questex, 1992
Physical Testing and Quality Control, Textile Institute, 1993.
Chemical Properties and Analysis, Textile Institute, 1994.
The Price for a Planet, Questex, 1996
Environmental Impact of Textiles: Production, Processes and Protection, Woodhead, 2003
Last Chance for Mankind, Questex, 2013
The Lives That I Have Lived, Questex, 2014
Making Textiles: A short history from prehistoric to present times, Questex, 2014
The Joys of ALS: finding happiness in a dark place, Questex, 2015

(plus about 300 articles in scientific Journals)

Fiction

Plays
Amnesty, Questex, 1996
Generation gap, Questex, 1996
Three one-act plays, Questex, 1996
Teacher's pet, Questex, 1996,
Two one-act plays, Questex, 1996
Independence Day, Questex, 1997
The holiday of your life, Questex, 1997

90

Where there's a will, Questex, 1999
Sleeping Beauty, Questex, 1999
Pink for a little girl, Questex, 1999
Christmas spirit, Questex, 1999
Murder takes a cruise, Questex, 2001
The magic cow, Questex, 2001
Funeral farce, Questex, 2002
The fine art of murder, Questex, 2003
Love and duty, Questex, 2003
Chimp, Questex, 2005
Undercover operation, Questex, 2005
Marauding, Questex, 2005
Not the same in wartime, Questex, 2006
Asylum, Questex, 2006
Aladdin and the magic lamp, Questex, 2008
New life for old, Questex, 2009
Mysterious visitors, 2011
Three for two, Questex, 2011
Forget the past, Questex, 2012
Evil forest, Questex, 2013
Writers in conflict, Questex, 2014
Drama in church worship, Questex, 2014
Shenanigans! Questex, 2015

Novels
The vultures of India, Questex, 2013
The wicked daughters of Portugal, Questex, 2013
The day of rest, Questex, 2013
The missing pharaoh, Questex, 2013
No Encores, Questex, 2013

Short story collections
Drama in life, Questex, 2012
On the lighter side, Questex, 2013
Adrift in the dark mind, Questex, 2013

54437120R00057

Made in the USA
Charleston, SC
31 March 2016